LLAMA DRAMA

REBECCA FELIX

Lerner Publications ◆ Minneapolis

Lerner Publications Company
An imprint of Lerner Publishing Group, Inc.
241 First Avenue North
Minneapolis, MN 55401 USA

For reading levels and more information, look up this title at www.lernerbooks.com.
Main body text set in Caecilia Com
Typeface provided by Monotype

Library of Congress Cataloging-in-Publication Data

Names: Felix, Rebecca, 1984– author.
Title: Llama drama / Rebecca Felix.
Description: Minneapolis, MN : Lerner Publications, [2021] | Series: Internet animal stars | Includes bibliographical references and index. | Audience: Ages 6–10. | Audience: Grades 2–3. | Summary: "Add a little drama with this guide to llamas! The fun, engaging design takes its inspiration from social media with text that informs young readers about their life cycle, habitat, and diet"— Provided by publisher.
Identifiers: LCCN 2019054994 (print) | LCCN 2019054995 (ebook) | ISBN 9781541597174 (library binding) | ISBN 9781728402895 (paperback) | ISBN 9781728400372 (ebook)
Subjects: LCSH: Llamas—Juvenile literature.
Classification: LCC QL737.U54 F45 2021 (print) | LCC QL737.U54 (ebook) | DDC 599.63/67—dc23

LC record available at https://lccn.loc.gov/2019051187
LC ebook record available at https://lccn.loc.gov/2019051188

Manufactured in the United States of America
1 – CG – 7/15/20

PAGE PLUS!

Scan QR codes throughout the book for videos of cute animals!

LLAMA DRAMA

What do you know about llamas? These wooly animals belong to the camel family. Llamas are domestic, which means they live with and around humans. And humans love llamas! The internet is full of wacky llama **content**. Learn basic llama facts. Then find out how these furry creatures gained fame online!

#LlamaLand

Llamas are native to South America.

#Llegit

Chapter 1

LLAMA LIFE

★ Little Llamas ★

Baby llamas are called crias (KREE-ahs). Newborn crias **vary** in size. They can weigh between 18 and 35 pounds (8 and 16 kg).

Crias are active soon after birth! They may walk and **nurse** within their first hour of life.

Crias nurse for six months. Then they become **independent**.

Scan this QR code to see a cria!

7

★ Llama Adults ★

Adult llamas are up to 6 feet (2 m) tall. They weigh up to 450 pounds (204 kg). Female llamas are usually smaller than males.

Crias grow for up to three years. After that, they are adults.

#LlamaCow

Llamas have thick, soft fur. It is often brown, but some llamas have black, white, or spotted fur.

9

★ Elder ★ Llamas

Because all llamas are domestic, people care for their basic needs.

People protect llamas from **predators** such as coyotes and cougars. The average llama lives about twenty years. But some live to be thirty years of age!

People keep llamas outdoors in many **climates**. Llamas need room to run and **graze**.

Scan this QR code to see a herd of llamas!

Chapter 2

PACK KNACK

Llamas also need grooming. Owners must trim the animals' toenails and **shear** their fur. Sometimes they turn llama fur into wool.

#FullWool

People raise llamas
for more than just fur.
Llamas are used to carry
supplies and goods.

Llamas are smart. Llamas are also well-behaved when they are treated kindly!

If a llama is mistreated, it may refuse to move. It may also hiss or spit at humans.

Llamas are able to learn tasks quickly.

Spitting is a form of llama **communication**. Llamas also hum and move their ears to communicate.

#SpitTake

Llamas are social animals. They do best when they live in a group.

Llamas also need a healthy diet. This includes fruits, vegetables, and grasses. Llamas produce and chew **cud** from these foods.

Scan this QR code to see a hungry llama!

Llamas also produce popular internet content! Gentle llamas charm the online world.

So do silly llamas, grumpy llamas, and happy llamas!

Chapter 3

LLAMAS IN POP CULTURE

The internet is packed with llama content! But how and why did these camel cousins become stars?

Researchers say it started with a children's book. *Llama Llama Red Pajama* by Anna Dewdney was published in 2005.

The book sold well. More *Llama Llama* books followed. These books helped make llamas popular.

Some researchers say the way that llamas look made these animals famous. Llamas have unique shaggy fur and long necks. The animals sometimes seem to smile.

Llamas also have funny personalities! Several **quirky**, funny, and even cranky llamas have become online royalty.

People relate to all these llama qualities.

#LlamaLlook

★ Llama Llegends ★

Most online llama content features nameless llamas. But some specific llamas became social media celebs!

#Lightning Llama
Llamas can run up to 35 miles (56 km) per hour!

Superstars! KAHKNEETA AND LANEY

On February 26, 2015, Kahkneeta and Laney got loose in Sun City, Arizona. Police tried to catch them. Footage of the llama chase went viral! The internet was full of llama memes, gifs, and hashtags that day.

MEME BREAK!

TRYING TO SMILE NATURALLY FOR SCHOOL PICTURES

WEARING A COOL NEW OUTFIT TO SCHOOL AND WAITING FOR THE COMPLIMENTS TO ROLL IN

WHEN YOUR TEACHER CALLS ON SOMEONE ELSE EVEN THOUGH YOU HAD YOUR HAND UP FIRST

LLAMAS ROCK!

Llamas aren't just celebrated online. They also appear on clothing, decorations, and more.

Interacting with llamas is popular too. In Texas, local llamas visit hospitals as therapy animals. And a North Carolina golf course employs a llama as a caddy!

Llamas are "lloved" around the world.

climate: the usual weather patterns of a place

communication: using words, sounds, or behaviors to exchange ideas

content: ideas, facts, and images available online

cud: a food that an animal brings back up from its stomach to chew again

graze: to eat plants that grow in a field

independent: not relying on others for support

nurse: to drink milk from a mother's body

predator: an animal that eats other animals to survive

quirky: unusual in an interesting or fun way

shear: to cut off an animal's wool or fur

vary: to be different

viral: spreading quickly to many people over the internet

WEBSITES

DK Find Out—Llama
https://www.dkfindout.com/us/animals-and-nature/camels/llama/
Learn how llamas help people do important tasks. Read how llamas' bodies help them survive in the mountains.

Heifer International—How to Tell the Difference Between Alpacas and Llamas
https://www.heifer.org/blog/alpacas-vs-llamas-how-to-tell-the-difference.html
Llamas are sometimes confused with alpacas! Learn about the differences between the animals here.

National Geographic Kids—Llama Drama
https://kids.nationalgeographic.com/explore/adventure_pass/amazing-animals/llama-drama/
Some llamas are protective of their owners. Read about the behavior of protective llamas.

BOOKS

Bodden, Valerie. *Llamas*. Mankato, MN: Creative Education, 2019.
Learn more about llamas and where they live. Then read a story from folklore explaining where llamas came from.

Dellaccio, Tanya. *Raising Llamas*. New York: PowerKids Press, 2020.
Learn how and why llamas are raised on farms, and explore more about the animal's characteristics.

Grunbaum, Mara. *Llamas*. New York: Children's Press, 2020.
Read about llamas and their history. Then learn more about how llamas communicate!